What the Aztecs Told Me

A GROUNDWOOD BOOK

Text and design copyright © 1994 by Krystyna Libura,
Ma. Cristina Urrutia and Claudia Burr
Translation copyright © 1997 by Groundwood Books Ltd.
Originally published in Mexico as *De lo que contaron al fraile*
by Ediciones Tecolote 1994
First English language edition 1997

The publisher gratefully acknowledges the assistance of
the Canada Council and the Ontario Arts Council.

Printed and bound in China by Everbest Printing Co

Groundwood Books / Douglas & McIntyre
585 Bloor Street West, Toronto, Ontario M6G 1K5

Distributed in the U.S.A. by Publishers Group West
4065 Hollis Street, Emeryville, CA 94608

Library of Congress data is available.

Canadian Cataloguing in Publication Data

Libura, Krystyna
    What the Aztecs told me
"A Groundwood book".
Translation of: De lo que contaron al fraile.
Spanish text based on Historia general de las cosas de Nueva
Espana in the Florentine Codex by Fray Bernardino de
Sahagun
ISBN 0-88899-305-6 (bound) ISBN 0-88899-306-4 (pbk.)
1. Aztecs - Juvenile literature. 2. Indians of Mexico - Juvenile
literature. I. Burr, Claudia. II. Urrutia, Ma. Cristina (Maria
Cristina). III. Aldana, Patricia, 1946- . IV. Sahagun,
Bernardino de, d. 1590. Historia general de las cosas de
Nueva Espana. V. Title.
F1219.L5813 1997   j972'.018   C97-930463-6

I, Bernardino de Sahagún, Spanish friar, came to Mexico in the sixteenth century as a missionary. For many years I met with the elders of the people who knew the language, beliefs and customs of their land. I have written down what they told me, so you could know how they lived before the Spaniards came.

What the Aztecs Told Me

Text and design by Krystyna Libura, Claudia Burr and Maria Cristina Urrutia

There was never a people so given over to their gods. They offered human sacrifices to them and even their own blood, piercing their skin with the thorns from the maguey plant as their god Quetzalcóatl had taught them to do.

All through the year the people held great feasts, dancing and singing to their gods, because they believed that the order of the universe and the life of man depended on it.

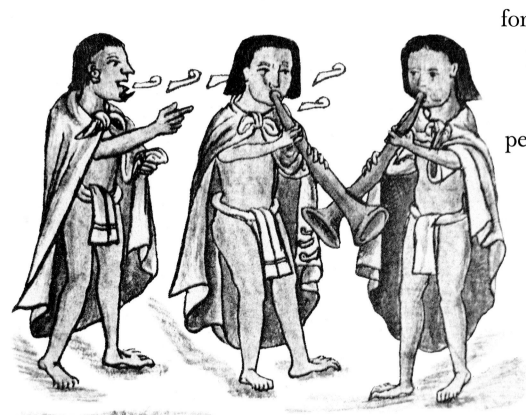

The feast of feasts was for the god Tezcatlipoca. For this occasion they chose a youth with a perfect body and taught him to play the flute.

For a whole year he was worshipped like a god. On the day of the feast he was taken to the temple. Alone he climbed the steps, breaking flutes as he went. At the top he was sacrificed by the high priests.

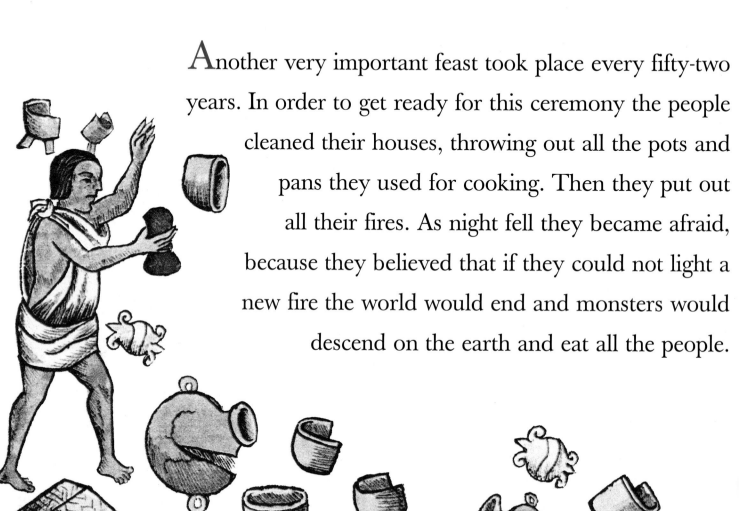

Another very important feast took place every fifty-two years. In order to get ready for this ceremony the people cleaned their houses, throwing out all the pots and pans they used for cooking. Then they put out all their fires. As night fell they became afraid, because they believed that if they could not light a new fire the world would end and monsters would descend on the earth and eat all the people.

At midnight the priests rubbed sticks of wood together to light a flame on the chest of a young man who had been sacrificed. This flame was carried from house to house, relighting all the fires, until night seemed like day.

Among the unusual beliefs of the land was the Ancient Mexicans' faith in the art of divination. The people would turn to the diviner to predict the future of newborn babies.

The diviners consulted a calendar, whose mysteries only they could decipher. Each day had a number and name of its own, such as One Ocelot, Three Eagle, Seven Rain or One Rabbit.

One Rabbit was considered a
lucky birthday. Those born on that
day would be hard workers.

And as long as they used their time wisely they would be rich and prosperous.

They told me about their forms of government. Their supreme lord was called the Tlatoani. He was so respected that no one dared to look upon his face. The Tlatoani had various responsibilities. He made sure that the fires burned continuously in the temples in honor of the gods.

The Tlatoani also looked after justice. He chose the noblest and wisest people to be judges. If the judges did not fulfill their duties they were put in cages and sentenced to death.

But the most important duty for the Tlatoani, given that the Ancient Mexicans were warriors, was the conduct of war. They made war not only to defend themselves but also to conquer far-off lands.

When they went to war they went in this order:

First the priests.

A day later the captains.

Finally the warriors.

A tribute was imposed on the conquered enemy. There were special days when the defeated peoples had to bring precious cloaks, feathered shields and rare foods to Tenochtitlan, the capital city.

There were also peaceful ways of obtaining precious and rare objects. Merchants, called pochtecas, brought  goods from far-off lands. The pochtecas carried heavy loads on their backs over great distances. Their voyages were dangerous since they often traveled through enemy territory. They acted as spies for the Tlatoani. This was how news came from afar.

The pochtecas brought feathers
from rare birds that they found
in hot countries. The great craftsmen in the capital made
beautiful cloaks, headdresses and shields from the feathers.

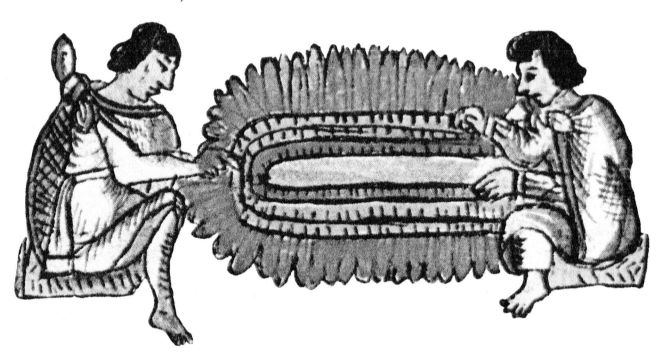

The Ancient Mexicans were proficient in other arts as well. They were great astronomers. They used the movement of the stars to measure time and used this calendar to count the passing years.

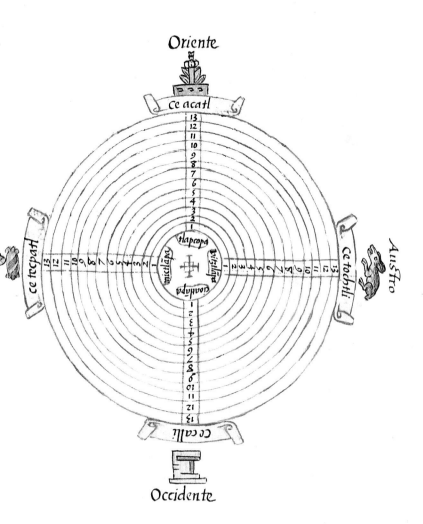

They were also healers. They knew the medicinal properties of roots, trees and stones. They could straighten broken bones and heal pain with herbal baths.

Because they understood the secrets of nature they were good fishermen and hunters.

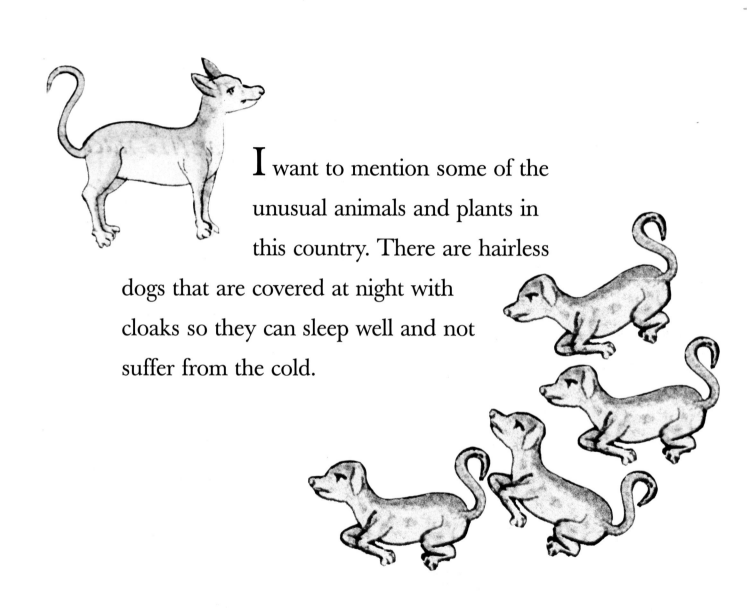

I want to mention some of the unusual animals and plants in this country. There are hairless dogs that are covered at night with cloaks so they can sleep well and not suffer from the cold.

In their houses the people keep
a strange kind of bird which they
eat. The males are called
guajolotes. They have big chests
and red wattles. Their heads turn
bright blue when they are angry.

Among the strange animals there is one called ayutochtli, "rabbit with a shell." It is, indeed, the size of a rabbit and seems to have armor. We call it an armadillo. The iguana is frightening because it looks like a dragon. It has scales and is as long as an arm.

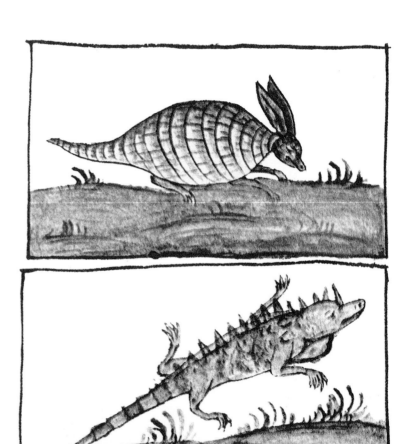

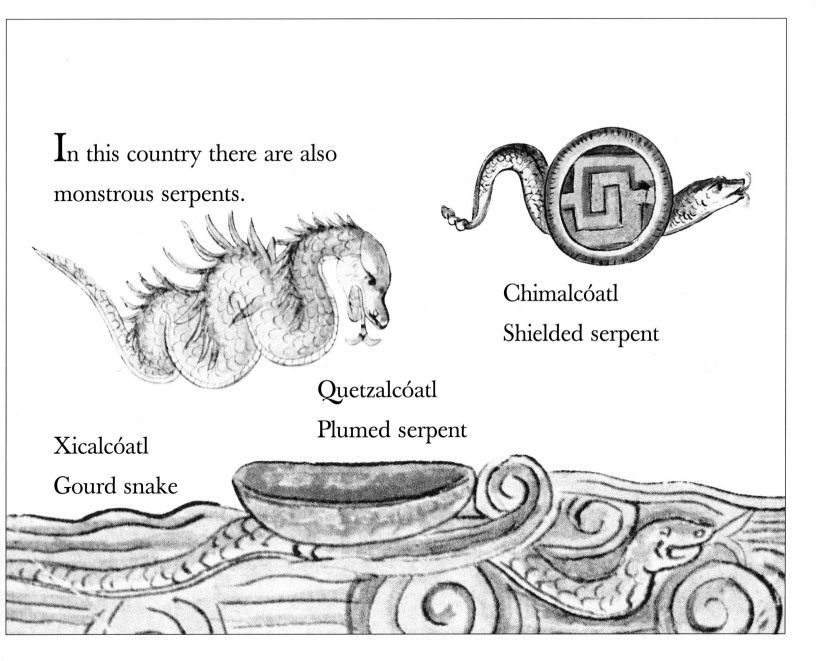

In this country there are also monstrous serpents.

Chimalcóatl
Shielded serpent

Quetzalcóatl
Plumed serpent

Xicalcóatl
Gourd snake

The plants are also marvelous, and many are unknown in the Old World. Here is a garden of fruit trees and various other plants:

Cocoa

Zapote

Yam

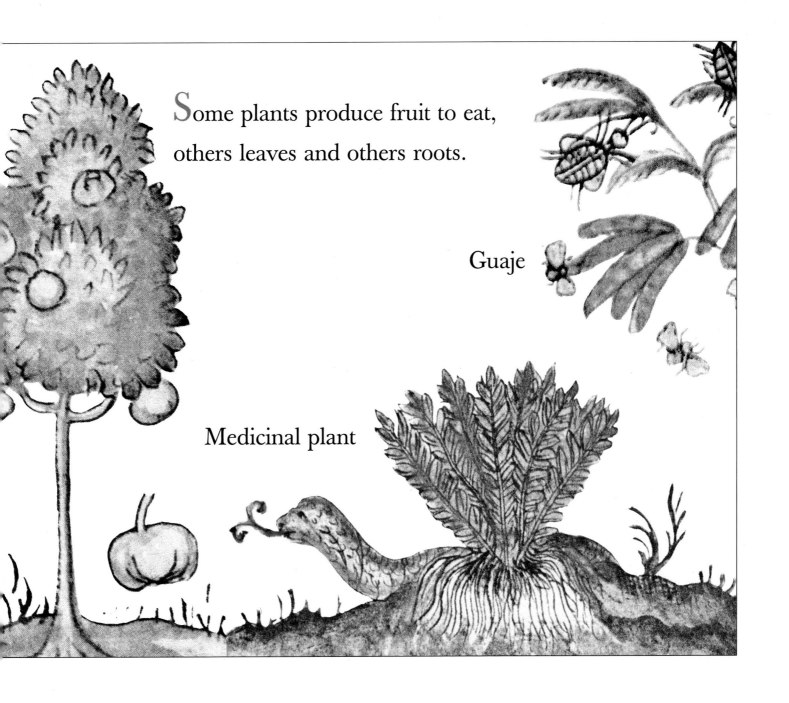

Some plants produce fruit to eat,
others leaves and others roots.

Guaje

Medicinal plant

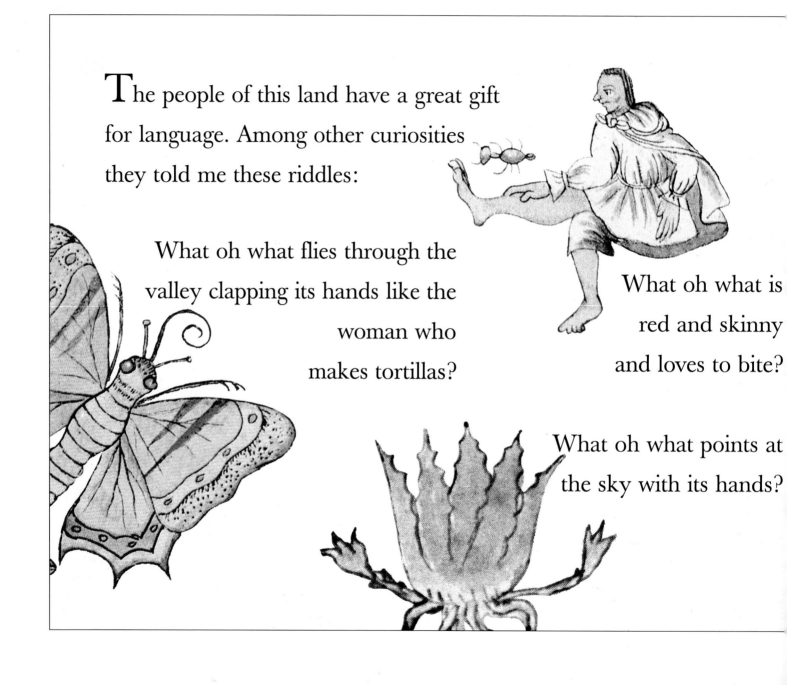

The people of this land have a great gift for language. Among other curiosities they told me these riddles:

What oh what flies through the valley clapping its hands like the woman who makes tortillas?

What oh what is red and skinny and loves to bite?

What oh what points at the sky with its hands?

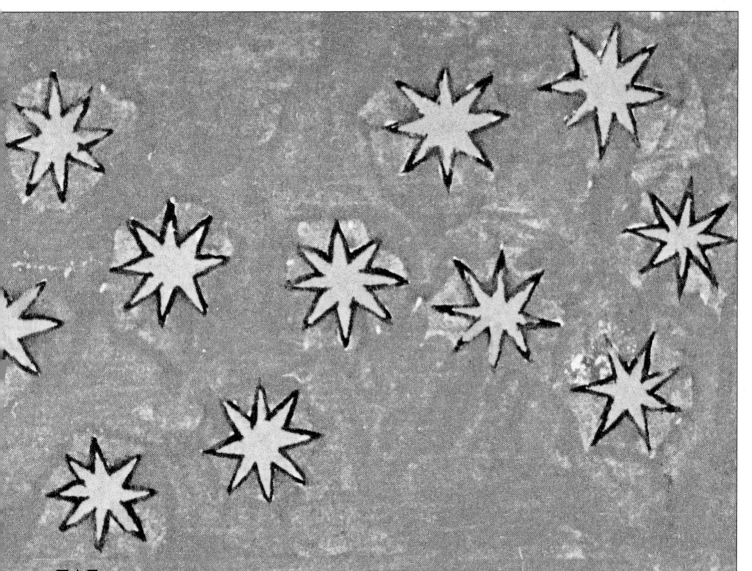

What oh what is a blue gourd spangled with toasted corn?

This book is based on a twelve-volume work by Friar Bernardino de Sahagún called *A General History of the Things of New Spain*, which was published in the sixteenth century. The drawings are from the manuscript version of the General History, which is known as the Florentine Codex. The culture and events that Friar Bernardino recorded had almost disappeared by the time he wrote his work. Only a few elders remained who could remember Mexico before the Spaniards arrived. It is thanks to them that we can glimpse this vanished world.

IMPORTANT TERMS AND DEFINITIONS

Ayutochtli—armadillo
Chimalcóatl, Xicalcóatl—mythical snakes
Guajolote—turkey
Guaje—a plant with seed pods
Maguey—a plant with sharp spiny leaves
Mexicas or Ancient Mexicans—while many native tribes were living in Mexico when the Spaniards came, the dominant group were the Aztecs, who called themselves Mexicas
Pochtecas—merchants or traders

Quetzalcóatl—a god who was represented as a plumed serpent
Tenochtitlan—the most important city of the Mexicas
Tlatoani—the supreme lord of the Mexicas; at the time of this story the Tlatoani was Moctezuma
Zapote—a fruit with sweet flesh (sapodilla)